ABOUT ME

for good fo
to eat and t
my childhood in Southern France, where family meals are the core of community and good food is a main topic of conversation.

In later life, whilst teaching in a Leicester Primary School, I discovered that many of our families had no idea how to cook basic meals, so I designed a developmental cookery curriculum and taught it to all of our pupils and invited their parents to weekly sessions to learn from their children.

Consequently, I have many years experience of simplifying recipes and ideas and making good food as accessible as possible, to as many people as I can reach.

My latest chapter comes as a result of scientific research into what really makes a healthy diet. I undertook ZOE testing (See p71 for more information) and discovered that I am much healthier and happier with more pulses and plants and less meat and dairy. I've combined this new information with my love of flavour, to adapt and invent all manner of recipes to make my diet as delicious, healthy and convenient as possible. Many of my recipes are from the internet or friends or adapted from things I already cooked, but I have combined them into this book, as a guide for easier ways to add really nutritious foods into your weekly routines.

Food for my body
Flavours textures, sights and smells
Food for my soul

CONTENTS

		Page
Ideas To Add Variety	Mixed Nuts	6
	Seed Mix	4
	Mega Salad	7
	Weekly Pulses	8
	Sprouts & Sprouting	8
	Stir Fry	10
	Seedy Crackers	11
	Hummus	12
	Pesto	12
	Soup	13
	Pearl Barley	14
	Herbs & Spices	14
	Vegetables	15
	Desserts	16
Ideas To Add Protein		17
Ideas for Avocados		19
Ideas for Gut Health		21
	Milk Kefir	23
	Sauerkraut	22
	Kimchi	24
Eating Out		25
Growing and Prepping		25
Planning		27
Recipes		28

RECIPES

		Veg/ Vegan	Freezes well	P
## Pulses				
Lentil Loaf	GF	Veg	❄	28
Falafel	GF/DF	Vegan	❄	29
Black Bean Burgers	GF/DF	Veg	❄	30
Hummus	GF/DF	Vegan	❄	31
Butter bean Mash/croquettes	GF/DF	Vegan	❄	32
Mixed Bean Salad	GF/DF	Vegan	❄	33
Mushroom and Chickpea Curry	GF/DF	Vegan	❄	34
Maharagwe – Kenyan Beans	GF/DF	Vegan	❄	35
## Main Dishes				
Seafood 'Risotto'	GF/DF			36
Lentil & Mushroom 'Risotto'	GF/DF	Vegan	❄	37
Seafood Pasta	GF/DF			38
Stir Fry/Air Fry	GF/DF	Vegan		39
Baked Fish	GF/DF			42
Chachouka With Eggs	GF/DF	Veg		43
Chicken Marinade	GF/DF			44
Salade Niçoise (Tuna)	GF/DF			45
Cauliflower/Macaroni Cheese	GF	Veg		46
## Vegetable Dishes				
Ratatouille	GF/DF	Vegan	❄	47
Easy Parmigiana Melanzane	GF	Veg		48
Courgetti Fastonara	GF	Veg		49
Courgette & Stilton Soup	GF	Veg	❄	50

Roasted Red Pepper & Tomato Soup	GF/DF	Vegan	❄	51
Frozen Pea & Mint Soup	GF/DF	Vegan	❄	52
Roast Mediterranean Vegetables	GF/DF	Vegan		53
Vegetable Stock Paste	GF	Veg	❄	54
Guacamole	GF/DF		❄	55

Dressings & Sauces

Vinaigrette	GF/DF	Vegan		56
Blender Mayonnaise	GF/DF	Veg		57
Cashew Mayonnaise	GF/DF	Vegan		58
Pesto	GF	Veg		59
Gremolata	GF/DF	Vegan		60
Romesco Sauce	GF/DF	Vegan	❄	61

Snacks

Spicy Chick Peas	GF/DF	Vegan		62
Seedy Crackers	GF/DF	Vegan		63
Chaffles	GF/DF	Veg	❄	64
Sweetcorn Pakora	GF/DF	Vegan	❄	65

Sweet

Tahini cookies	GF/DF	Vegan	66
Flaxseed and Chocolate cookies	GF/DF	Vegan	67
Almond Flour Pancakes	GF	Vegan	68

Appendix 1, 2 & 3	69
Appendix 4	70
About ZOE Testing	71

Ideas To Add Variety

Recent research shows that eating a variety of plants is really beneficial for your gut microbiome and your general health. The different phytonutrients feed different parts of our physiology and can even reduce the chance of bowel cancer. In even better news, this not only includes vegetables and legumes but also herbs, spices & grains!

The current recommendation is to aim for 30 different plants a week. I know that sounds like a lot, but here are some ideas that will help you to increase your tasty plant intake.

Mega Salad

One of my favourite things to eat is a big salad, either on its own or added to my main meal.

I start with a variety of 'bases' that range from a shop bought herb salad bag or mixed leaves, watercress or rocket, through to home-grown herbs & leaves in summer and home-grown sprouts all year (See p8 for a guide to easy sprouting). I can grow 3 types of sprout at a time, so that's a tasty start!

I then add whatever fresh vegetables are available. This can be cucumber, celery, tomatoes, peppers, courgettes (in cubes or ribbons), carrots (grated or in ribbons), shredded cabbage, avocado & even left over cooked vegetables, like potatoes or peppers.

I keep lots of salad 'extras' in the fridge, such as capers, pitted olives, sun-dried tomatoes, gherkins & artichokes. Any jarred antipasti make a tasty addition to a salad.

So I chop everything up, mix it all together and top it with a dressing (see p56-61) and a big handful of seed mix!

For a main course, I add one of my protein options from the next section.

Nut Mix

I keep a container of mixed nuts handy. I use an old yoghurt pot, but any tub or bag will do. I buy big bags of a variety of nuts, including pecans, hazelnuts, peanuts, cashews & almonds & add 2 handfuls of each to my pot. Give the pot a shake to mix them & then add them to whatever I'm eating.

They're great as a snack & are super portable. They're also very tasty as a topping for a salad or dessert. You can chop them up a bit if you prefer.

Seed Mix

I keep a container of seed mix handy, a jam jar or any tub or bag will do. I buy big bags of a variety of seeds, including sesame, sunflower, pumpkin, chia, & pine nuts (toasted at home), and add 2 handfuls of each to my pot. Give the pot a shake to mix them & then add them to whatever I'm eating. They're great as a topping for a salad, cooked vegetables or dessert.

My favourite way to serve vegetables is steamed, tossed in extra virgin olive oil (EVOO) & sprinkled with seeds & bagel seasoning.

Weekly Pulse 💓

Every weekend, I pressure cook a cup of beans or lentils. I use an Instant Pot (See Appendix 4), but you can just boil them if you don't have a pressure cooker.

While they're still warm, I drain them & grate in a clove or two of garlic, add 2 tablespoons of Extra Virgin Olive Oil, 1 tablespoon of vinegar or lemon juice, salt & pepper & a spice or two – often it's cumin, or celery salt, sometimes it's sumac or smoked paprika, whatever looks good at the time. I then pop them into two takeaway tubs – one for the fridge & one for the freezer. These are then available to add to whatever I eat throughout the week.

Sprouts & Sprouting

I'm sure you're familiar with the bean sprouts that are used in Chinese recipes (mung beans), well it turns out you can sprout all sorts of beans & lentils really easily at home. Not only are they tasty & crunchy, they also each have a different blend of super healthy nutrients. What I love most about them, is how convenient and cheap they are, compared to bagged salad from the shops.

You can sprout any beans or lentils that haven't been processed or split. My favourites are lentils, broccoli & mung beans. You'll be surprised how easy it is.

What You'll Need

- A clean glass jar with a lid
- Some raw unprocessed lentils, mung beans or broccoli seeds
- A sieve or tea strainer

Sprouting Method

1) Take 25g (a handful) of lentils, beans or seeds & put them in the jar with plenty of water. Rest the lid on top of the jar.

2) Leave to soak overnight.

3) Next morning, sieve them, fill the jar with fresh water to rinse them, sieve them again and leave them damp. Pop the lid loosely on the jar & store in a dark place.

4) Later that day, rinse again and leave damp again.
5) Repeat steps 3 & 4 for 4 or 5 days until they have sprouted!

It's that easy!

If you get really keen, you can buy sprouting kits online, that have trays, so you can grow a variety of sprouts in the same kit. These are just as easy to use, and are even self draining. You just add 500ml of water to the top layer, twice a day & empty the collection tray at the bottom (I use it to water plants).

How To Store & Eat Your Sprouts

When you're happy with how big they are, you can transfer them to the fridge to stop them growing. I keep mine in a plastic container, with a piece of kitchen roll in the bottom. No need for a lid, but you can add one if you like.

You can eat them as snacks (I like mine with some salt & smoked paprika), as a base for a salad, or on top of other dishes, as a garnish. Alfalfa or boccoli sprouts are peppery & great mixed with some sesame seeds. You can also cook with them. The mung sprouts are particularly good in a stir fry.

Stir Fry/Air Fry

Stir fries are a great way to get plenty of variety into a main dish. This is not exactly a recipe book, but more of a guide, so I'm just going to suggest all sorts of things that you could include and you can choose the ones you like!

The main trick with stir fries is to cut everything roughly the same size, & quite thinly, so that it all cooks quickly. All the ingredients, except meat, fish or seafood, can be eaten raw, so only need a light cooking to add some flavour.

You can add a simple sauce of soy sauce or coconut aminos (a similar tasting, but non soy sauce), sesame oil & Chinese 5 spice seasoning. I like to top mine with toasted sesame seeds, chopped peanuts or cashews, some chopped coriander & a drizzle of toasted sesame oil. See p39 For ingredients and methods.

Seedy Crackers

These crackers are seeds and chickpea flour, with some seasoning, spices and yeast flakes for extra flavour.

See p64 for the recipe.

It's worth making a big batch of these, as they are really tasty & go really well with hummus, guacamole and cheese. Store them in an air tight container and in theory they will last a few weeks.

Hummus

Hummus is traditionally a simple mixture of cooked, peeled chickpeas, olive oil, tahini (sesame seed paste), garlic, lemon juice, salt & pepper. Shop bought hummus is good but home made is better and SO easy! It also freezes really well.

There are lots of varieties of hummus available these days & you can actually make a version with all sorts of different pulses. I also don't bother to peel mine. I'm happy with the coarser texture.
See p31 for a basic hummus recipe.

Ideas for Hummus Varieties

1. Try any other type of cooked pulse, such as canellini beans, black beans or lentils.
2. Try a vegetable as the base, such as cooked carrot, sweet potato, beetroot or roasted red peppers. You can mix them with a pulse or make a separate kind of dip altogether.
3. Try any nut butter in place of the tahini: peanut butter, macadamia, almond... whatever you like!
4. Try adding chopped, soft fresh herbs like coriander, parsley or chives.
5. Try adding traditional spices like sumac, smoked paprika or cumin, or even chilli if you like it hot. (Fresh or dried are both good). I like to mix them into the blend and also sprinkle a little on top for garnish.
6. Try topping the finished hummus with a good glug of EVOO (extra virgin olive oil) and some toasted pine nuts, cashews, peanuts or sesame seeds, pistachio or a swirl of harissa to spice it up.

Pesto

Pesto, like hummus, has a traditional form and many, many tasty varieties.

Traditional pesto is pine nuts, basil, parmesan, olive oil & garlic (& it's delicious!), but you can change up the herb and nut elements, use nutritional yeast flakes in place of the parmesan and add all sorts of other flavours.

You can use it as a dip or add it to cooked pasta. It's also nice on top of a salad or as a topping on fish.

11

Ideas for Pesto Varieties

1. Use any soft green leaves in place of the basil, such as parsley, coriander, chives, rocket, watercress, mint and even cooked peas, in any combination!
2. Use another type of nut or seed in place of the pine nuts: sunflower or pumpkin seeds work well, as do cashews, walnuts or almonds.
3. Swap out the parmesan for feta or soft goat's cheese, or 2 tsp of nutritional yeast flakes for a vegan version. You may want to add a squeeze of lemon juice to adjust the flavour. See what you think.
4. Change the seasonings to something more punchy, such as smoked paprika or cayenne, sumac or cumin.

Hey Pesto.

- 2 packed cups of mixed fresh tender herbs or greens, such as basil, parsley, arugula, kale, or spinach
- 1/4 cup freshly grated hard aged cheese, such as Parmesan or pecorino, OR 1/4 cup nutritional yeast
- 1/4 cup nuts or seeds, such as pine nuts, walnuts, cashews, or sunflower seeds
- 2 cloves garlic
- 1/3 cup extra virgin olive oil
- 2-3 Tbsp lemon juice
- 3-6 Tbsp water

Ideas from ZOE

Soup

You can make soup out of just about anything, but with a good recipe, you can make really tasty soup.
Research shows that smooth, blended soups cause a higher glucose response than more chunky ones, as the 'sugars' in the ingredients have been broken down, so are more available. I like my soup chunky, but you can blend yours however you like.

To make any soup, fry some onions and maybe garlic in a little oil, add vegetables cut into small, even pieces, add water or stock, boil for 15 minutes, blend and season. That really is how easy it is. So you could do this with any vegetables that you have, then season with your favourite spices to give it some extra zing.

For my favourite soup recipes see p50-52

Pearl or Pot Barley

I have been using pearl barley instead of rice, to accompany dishes like curry and chilli. It is far more fibrous than even brown rice and also has much more protein. I love the nutty texture and have been batch cooking it in stock to freeze in individual portions.

Another great use for barley is in a kind of risotto.

For my favourite 'risotto' recipes see p36 & p37.

Herbs & Spices

Herbs & spices really are a matter of taste. There are SO many to choose from, with such different flavour profiles.

Fresh herbs can be added to many dishes to give them a lift. In summer I like to use mixed fresh herb leaves as a base for a salad. They're also great as a finely chopped garnish for a dish, whether it's meat fish or vegetables. It's fun to experiment with them and see what you like.

It's easy to grow parsley, coriander, chives, basil and mint on a windowsill at home.

One really punchy way to add herby flavour is a gremolata, See p60 for my recipe.

My favourite spices are cumin & smoked paprika, but I also love celery seed, sumac & ground coriander. There are so many to choose from and until you've tasted them,

it's difficult to know if you want to add them to your foods.

You could start by trying blends, like fajita blend, ras al hanout, garam masala or curry powder. Just check that they don't contain any unnecessary additives.

Vegetables

I'm sure you already eat all sorts of vegetables, but in order to increase the variety, I invite you to have a look at ones you've never eaten before. If you're lucky enough to live near a city, chances are there are some shops selling interesting vegetables like kohlrabi, celeriac or cocoyam. During lockdown, I had an organic vegetable box delivered, and tasted some really interesting, locally grown vegetables that I'd never tried before.

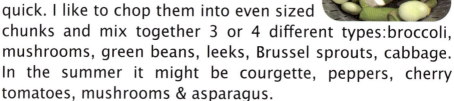

My favourite ways of cooking and serving vegetables are really simple & quick. I like to chop them into even sized chunks and mix together 3 or 4 different types: broccoli, mushrooms, green beans, leeks, Brussel sprouts, cabbage. In the summer it might be courgette, peppers, cherry tomatoes, mushrooms & asparagus.

I then either steam them for 10 minutes or toss them in some olive oil & air fry them for 10 minutes. Both ways are quick and tasty. I serve them with some more olive oil, salt & pepper and maybe slithers of almonds or more often Bagel Seasoning (see Appendix1 for suppliers).

Desserts

I don't have a sweet tooth, so I'm afraid this section is a bit thin. My current favourite dessert is Greek yoghurt with mixed berries (fresh in summer, frozen in winter) and a sprinkle of my seed mix on top. I sometimes add a drizzle of vanilla essence or a grating of dark chocolate.

I am however really enjoying the flaxseed cookies that ZOE posted on their Instagram page. The recipe calls for them to be rolled into balls, but I have found that I can line a brownie tin with parchment paper and spread the mixture evenly with a spoon. This makes it much quicker, easier and cleaner. I keep them in an airtight tin & tell everyone that they're healthy, so that they last a few more days!
See p67 for the recipe.

I love to eat well
Arousing all my senses
A gift of good health

IDEAS TO ADD PROTEIN

The importance of protein has been much discussed in recent years. I'm not a scientist or a dietitian, so I choose to trust my body's requests for protein. The Protein Leverage Hypothesis suggests that our bodies know when they've had enough protein. You're likely to still feel hungry, until your protein needs have been met. My preferences for protein sources have changed a lot in the last year. My body seems much happier with pulses, eggs, fish, seafood and birds (chicken, turkey, pheasant, partridge, pigeon) rather than red meat.

Eggs are great parcels of protein – quick and easy!

- Fry a couple in extra virgin olive oil to pop on top of any dish.
- Keep a few soft boiled in the fridge, for snacks or to add to a meal.
- Bake in bites or mini crustless quiches, great as breakfast, snacks or in packed lunches.
- An omelette is a super speedy high protein meal: add mushrooms, cheese, herbs, spinach or cooked vegetables. (See my 'How To' film on my Fresher Bites YouTube channel).

Pulses – Beans & Lentils

I've always liked pulses, but I'm finding that with a little imagination they can be made extra delicious.

My main way of eating them is my weekly pulses, as mentioned on p8. I add a portion of them to most of my meals, as a tasty side.

As also mentioned previously (p8) pulses can easily be sprouted, which adds great crunch to a meal. They only take a few days to sprout, even in winter in England, so make for an easily available salad base.

I have quite a few recipes in the pulses section which are made from red lentils & chickpea flour, both of which lend themselves to replacing wheat flour surprisingly well. (See p28-35)

The hummus varieties on p12 are a great way of adding protein to a meal. A bowl served with celery, carrot & red pepper strips to dip makes a great starter or snack. A big blob with a salad is also delicious.

Butter beans make a surprisingly tasty replacement for mashed potatoes, and contain much more fibre and protein. Serve it as a side, make into a patty & fry, or as a topping for a fish or shepherd's pie.

A great way of adding some pulses to more traditional meals is to add a handful (40 gms) of red or green lentils, and 75ml of extra liquid to dishes such as Spaghetti Bolognese, meat stew or any other 'saucy' dish. The lentils will cook away to nothing, thicken the sauce and add some extra protein, which will enable you to reduce the meat content.

A surprising way to change the protein source in a cheese sauce is to mix silken tofu & a little chick pea flour with cheddar cheese, season & gently heat. – voila! This sauce has far more fibre and much less carbohydrate and is great poured over vegetables, whole cauliflower or cooked macaroni. (see P46 for recipe)

Meat, Fish, Seafood, Birds & Game.

I'm eating less of this kind of protein but enjoying a small portion as part of a meal. For recipes see p38-45

Ideas for Snacks

My focus here is to move away from deep fried carbs (mmmm) and to eat more whole foods as snacks.

Nuts make a delicious snack and are easy to carry around. You can always add some spicy seasonings to them to make them even more tasty.

The seedy crackers on p64 are also great snacks on their own or dipped in hummus or pesto.

For other ideas see the snack section on p63

IDEAS FOR AVOCADOS

Well, it turns out, after all those years of avoiding their fat little bodies, that avocados are a fabulous food!

Yes, they are high in fat, but not only is it 'good fat' but it's packaged with lots of fibre and nutrients that make them really good for us!

Whilst wearing a blood glucose monitor, I tested out the theory, that eating an avocado would lessen the glucose spike of something high carb eaten with or after it. It's definitely true! So I can eat bread or toast (preferably a very seedy slice), with avocado smeared all over it & the bread doesn't cause me an unhealthy glucose response!

Hooray for avocados!

Use them as butter, eat them as they are, add them to everything!

We have taken to sharing one to start our dinner most days.

Toppings for avocados:

- olive oil & bagel seasoning
- salt
- lemon juice
- balsamic vinegar
- a pinch of paprika
- sesame seeds & soy sauce (or coconut aminos)
- Homemade mayonnaise – see p57
- Pesto – see p59
- Gremolata – see p60

Another fabulous way to eat avocados is as **guacamole.** This vibrant green dip can be smeared on toast, served with salad, as a side dish a snack or a starter. It's great with seedy crackers or raw vegetables. It also freezes really well, as long as you ensure there's no air in with it, by covering it with a sheet of baking paper or cling film..

See my Basic Guacamole Recipe on P55

Storing Avocados

We all know how sneaky avocados are, and what a challenge it is to eat them while they are ripe.

My first trick is to buy unripe, hard avocados and put them with some ripe bananas. Within 2 or 3 days they become perfectly ripe. (There's some gassy scientific reason for it!)

My next trick is 2 ways of storing them. One is to store the whole, unpeeled avocado fully submerged in water in the fridge. They take up a bit of room, but they will keep for a week or two! I guess there's another gassy scientific explanation for that, too.

Another option that I've found very successful

is to peel and quarter them (easier than halving) & freeze the quarters on a tray. The next day, you can bag them up in portions. (I vacuum seal mine). They do get a little softer once defrosted, but they are perfectly good enough to eat 'au naturel', as long as you don't leave them for too long.

I have recently enjoyed being able to buy some organic avocados from a Crowd Farming group in Spain. See Appendix1 on P69

19

IDEAS FOR BETTER GUT HEALTH

Our guts thrive on variety, especially **plant variety**. Different beneficial gut bugs prefer different plants and fibres, so the wider variety that we consume, the better range of bugs we feed & encourage. Fermented foods are also good for introducing more helpful bugs.

You can buy fermented foods, but often they have been pasteurised, so the good bugs have been killed off.

Fermented foods found in the chilled section are more likely to still have live cultures, but the best way to be sure of them is to make your own. For all your fermenting needs, there's a fantastic Facebook Group called **UK Fermenting Friends**. You can get starters from group members and they are an absolute fount of knowledge and experience.

Milk Kefir is a really easy place to start.

You'll need:
1Tbs milk kefir grains,
2 glass jars
250 ml fresh milk
a small sieve or tea strainer

1. Pop the grains & milk into the jar
2. Leave covered for 3 days (in the fridge or on the worktop).
3. Strain the kefir into the second jar & store in the fridge
4. Replace the grains into the jar and add more fresh milk to the grains & start the process again.

It really is that simple!

I keep mine at the front of the fridge so it doesn't get too cold (If it gets too cold the grains can stop working).

You can make it on the counter or in the fridge. I find it too sour if I make it at room temperature. You can also leave it longer for a sharper taste and thicker kefir. I use full fat goat milk & give my dogs a teaspoon each a day. It seems to prevent itchiness.

There's never any need to rinse the grains. The gluey coating that appears is kefiran and you want that. The grains will multiply and within a few weeks, you'll be able to give a friend a tablespoon of them to start their own process.

Sauerkraut is also very easy but takes a little longer.
You will need:
- a large clean bowl
- accurate weighing scales
- a large clip top glass jar (1 or 2 Litre Kilner type)
- a large white cabbage
- Sea salt or rock salt (20g per kilo)
- * 1/2 tsp Caraway seeds – optional
- * 1/2 tsp Black peppercorns –optional

Sauerkraut Method

1. Take off a clean outer cabbage leaf and save for later.
2. Shred the rest of the cabbage into even sized slices & weigh it.
3. Weigh out the salt at 2% (see table below)
4. In the large bowl, massage the salt into the cabbage and break the cabbage down with your hands or even bash it with a rolling pin. You want it to be really soft, so massage for at least 10 minutes.
5. Squash the cabbage very firmly into your jar, ensuring that there are no air pockets (these would harbour mould), and pour all the briny liquid on top.

6. Squash everything down firmly, ensuring that all the cabbage is under the brine.
7. Use your saved cabbage leaf to cover the whole mixture, ensuring that it stays well below the brine.
8. Use a glass ramekin or fermenting weight to keep everything under the brine.

9. Close the jar and place it in a large bowl (to collect any leakage)somewhere dark for 2-6 weeks, until bubbling subsides. The design of the clip top hinge will allow the gasses to release, without letting any mould spores in.
10. Open the jar VERY CAREFULLY as it may spurt. Taste the sauerkraut and decide if it is sour enough for your taste. If so, move it to the fridge. If not, close it and leave it for another few days.

Cabbage	Salt
Per each 100g	2g
500g	10g
1 Kg	20g
1.5 Kg	30g
2 Kg	40g

Kimchi is my absolute favourite. It's a bit more work, but so worth it. I tend to make it in large quantities, as it keeps forever.

Equipment
- A large clean bowl
- A food processor
- A large clip top glass jar (2 -5 Litre Kilner type)

Ingredients
- 2 heads of Chinese leaf (Napa cabbage)
- 2 big garlic cloves chopped,
- 6 tsp ginger grated
- 6 spring onions chopped finely
- 2 small carrots grated
- a shake of white sugar (2 tsp)
- 2.5 Tbs Korean red pepper powder
- 3 tbs fish sauce (optional)

Kimchi Method

1. Make a 10% brine. (200g salt per litre of water)
2. Chop the cabbage into 3cm pieces & cover with the brine. Leave for 2 hours to wilt.
3. Meanwhile roughly chop the spring onions & carrots.
4. Blitz all the other ingredients to a paste in a food processor.
5. Rinse & drain the cabbage & combine well with the other ingredients. Massage everything together and make sure the paste coats everything.
6. Pack it all tightly into the jar, making sure nothing sticks out above the paste. You may want to use a ramekin or weight to keep everything below the liquid.
7. Cover & leave in a warm, dark place for 2 weeks.
8. Taste & decide whether to continue the fast fermentation or to put it in the fridge to continue to ferment more slowly.

For lots of tips on how to make traditional kimchi, see Maangchi on YouTube.

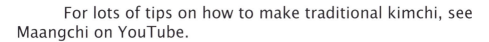

Sour dough Bread is another lovely wild ferment to make. The cooking of the bread kills the active 'bugs' but

they then become a pre-biotic, which feeds the bugs that already live in your intestines. It's really easy to make and keep your own sour dough starter. I recommend Elaine Boddy's books, Facebook group & YouTube channel for all your sour dough needs. See Appendix 2

23

IDEAS FOR EATING OUT

I love eating out. It's my favourite thing to do. What I eat has changed in the last year, since following ZOE guidance (see p71) and I've found some delicious new plant based dishes from a simple change in my attitude towards them!

If I don't see anything plant based that I fancy, or I just fancy some meat or fish, I order it with extra vegetables & often without the simple carb (rice, chips, bread).

I read menus differently now, as I'm looking for a variety of vegetables. Most restaurants are happy to mix & match or to add extra vegetables to any dish.

Growing & Prepping

On p8 I showed you how easy it is to **grow sprouts** at home. It's also easy to grow salad leaves and you can get great starter kits from companies like Getting People Growing.

If you're feeling more ambitious, you can buy herb & salad seeds & plant them in a window box. They should be successful throughout Spring & Summer. Chillis grow well, too.

My **weekly pulses** (p8) are a great way to prepare ahead, to enable you to add some tasty plants to any meal.

I also keep jars of **salad 'extras'** in the fridge, so that even when I don't have salad leaves, I have some plants to make some kind of salad with. You can even add things like olives, capers & mixed seeds to a bowl of cubed boiled potatoes.

Freezing in single portions makes it really easy to add variety to a meal.

You can freeze individual portions of:

- Cooked Pearl or Pot Barley
- Guacamole
- Hummus
- Pesto
- Butter bean mash
- Lentil Loaf (slices)
- Falafel (raw or cooked)
- Cooked beans or lentils
- Ratatouille
- Chachouka base
- Barley 'Risotto'
- Mushroom & Chickpea Curry
- Romesco sauce
- Maharagwe
- Soup
- Mixed vegetables – leftovers or pre frozen
- Cooked Pakora

You can also freeze vegetable scraps for making into vegetable stock paste. I keep an open tub in a freezer drawer and throw in trimmings and scraps every time I cook. Every now and then, when I've got enough, I make vegetable stock paste and freeze that! See the recipe on p54

25

IDEAS FOR PLANNING

(Things that have really helped me)

1. Make an appointment with yourself. Set a date and time to choose what you're going to batch cook or prepare ahead. Set a date and time to cook it. Gift yourself the time you need to make changes and improvements to what you eat.

2. Get everything ready before you start the job. You can even assemble all the equipment and then go and do something else for a while. When you come to do the job, it's ready to go. In my experience, it makes it far less daunting.

3. On Sunday, choose a new dish that you are going to make next week. Pick an evening that you are going to make it and make sure that you buy what you need before hand. By making an appointment with yourself, you're committing to giving yourself the time and making sure you get it done.

LENTIL LOAF
20 slices

Ingredients

- 2 cups (400g) dry red lentils
- 3 eggs
- 200g yoghurt
- 50 ml extra virgin olive oil
- 5g bicarbonate of soda
- 10g baking soda
- 200g feta cheese, cubed
- a handful of finely chopped dill
- 2 tsp cumin
- salt & pepper
- sesame seeds to garnish

a large mixing bowl
a food processor
spatula
1lb loaf or cake tin

This recipe is high protein, high fibre, low carb, really good for your gut and really tasty too!

Method

1. Soak the lentils for 2-3 hours in 1.5l water
2. Drain and add the eggs, yoghurt (room temp) & olive oil,
3. Blend
4. Add bicarb, baking powder, feta & seasonings and stir.
5. Pour into an oiled tin & top with sesame seeds.
6. Bake at 180°C (356°F) for 25 -30 mins, until a skewer comes out clean.
7. Leave to cool.
8. Slice with a sharp knife and enjoy fresh or freeze slices separately and reheat by frying in extra virgin olive oil.

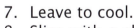

* It may take longer to bake, depending on the shape of your tin.

FALAFEL
approx 60 pieces – freezes well

Ingredients

- 500g dried chickpeas (soaked overnight)
- 1 small onion
- 4 cloves garlic
- 25g fresh parsley leaves
- 10g fresh coriander
- 2 Tbsp chick-pea flour
- 2 tsp salt
- 2 tsp ground cumin
- 1 tsp ground coriander
- ½ tsp ground cardamom
- ¼ tsp ground black pepper
- ¼ tsp cayenne pepper
- 1 tsp baking powder
- oil for frying

Equipment

Food processor
Large bowl
*Falafel shaper (optional)

Method

1. Peel and quarter the onion and blend with the peeled garlic cloves.
2. Add all the other ingredients & blend, scrape, stir and repeat four times until you have the correct consistency. You want it to be a rough paste, still with some texture.
3. Transfer to a bowl, cover and refrigerate for a minimum of 1 hour, to firm up.
4. When ready to make the falafels, use an ice-cream scoop or spoon to portion a tablespoon of mixture. Use wet hands to form balls & then gently flatten them. Or use a falafel shaper if you have one.
5. Heat enough oil to cover half of each falafel, so that you only need to turn it once The amount you use will depend on the size of your pan and your falafel.
6. Fry for around 2-3 minutes each side until a golden brown colour. These freeze well both raw and cooked.

BLACK BEAN BURGERS
Makes 4 very filling burgers

Ingredients

- 50g smooth peanut butter
- 250g of cooked black beans
- 2 peeled cloves of garlic
- 2 tsp chilli flakes
- 1 tsp ground cumin
- 1 Tbsp olive oil
- 1 heaped Tbsp chick-pea flour
- 1 lime, zest only
- 1 tsp sea salt flakes
- 1 egg
- 250g chestnut mushrooms

To serve

- 1 lime, cut into 4 wedges
- A handful of chopped salted peanuts
- A handful of chopped fresh coriander

Equipment

Food processor
Large bowl

Method

1. Put the peanut butter, 100g of the black beans, the garlic, chilli flakes, cumin, olive oil, flour, lime zest, sea salt flakes and egg into a food processor and blitz until you have a very thick paste. Tip it into a large bowl and stir in the rest of the black beans.
2. Tip the mushrooms into the processor – no need to wash the bowl – and pulse until you have a **dry** mushroom mince. Stir this into the black bean mixture.
3. With damp hands, form it into four thick burgers and arrange them on a lined baking sheet.
4. Bake in the oven at 180°C fan/200°C for 25-30 minutes. When they've got 10 minutes left, gently flip them over so they can crisp up on the other side.
5. Top with a handful of chopped peanuts and coriander & serve with a lime wedge.

HUMMUS

Ingredients

- 240g cooked chick peas (a drained tin or cook your own)
- 1 clove garlic
- 4 Tbs Extra Virgin Olive Oil
- 2 Tbs tahini
- 1/2 tsp salt
- 1/2 tsp pepper
- Juice of a lemon

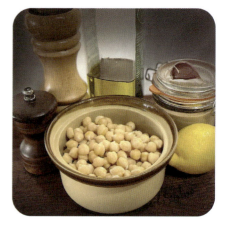

Equipment

Food processor/blender

Notes

For ideas for varieties of hummus, see P12

Method

1. Place all ingredients in a blender.
2. Blend until you reach your preferred texture.
3. Depending on your machine, you will probably need to scrape down to incorporate the unblended parts.
4. You can also add a little warm tap water to loosen the mixture, depending how you like it.
5. Store in the fridge or freezer.
6. Serve with raw vegetable batons or the crackers from p63.

BUTTER BEAN MASH/CROQUETTES
4 servings

Ingredients

Per portion:

- 240g cooked butter beans
  (I like to cook mine in vegetable stock, but tinned & drained are also fine).
- 2 tsp extra virgin olive oil
- Salt & Pepper to taste
* A beaten egg & breadcrumbs (optional)

Equipment

a fork, masher or blender

Notes

* For pressure cooking times for various beans, see Appendix 4 on P69

Method

1. Mix the beans & oil together and mash to your preferred texture, seasoning as you go. add a splash of water if you want it smoother.

2. You can serve as it is or make the mash into small patties, coat them in beaten egg & breadcrumbs and shallow fry them, for delicious, filling croquettes. For this you will want a drier mixture.

3. The mash and cooked croquettes freeze and defrost well.

31

NOTATO SALAD

Ingredients

- 250g butter beans
- 2 spring onions
- 1 stalk celery
- 2 Tbs Greek Yoghurt
- 2 Tbs Mayonnaise (see P57)
- salt & pepper to taste
- Finely chopped fresh mint
- A sprinkle of sumac

Equipment

sharp knife
large bowl
mixing spoon

Notes

This super-quick salad makes a great party dish & travels well.

Method

1. Strain the beans and discard the liquid.
2. Finely chop the spring onions & celery
3. Mix all the ingredients together and season to taste.
4. Add a sprinkle of sumac or a squeeze of lemon to taste.

   * For pressure cooking times for various beans, see Appendix 4 on P69

MUSHROOM AND CHICKPEA CURRY
Serves 2

Ingredients

- 1 onion
- 1 clove garlic
- 100g mushrooms
- 2 x15ml spoons curry paste
- 2 x15ml spoons tomato puree
- 240g cooked chickpeas
- 1 400ml can coconut milk
- 1 x 15ml spoon oil

Equipment
Chopping board, sharp knife, weighing scales, saucepan, measuring jug, measuring spoons, colander.

Notes
You can use curry paste or a tablespoon of your favourite curry powder.

Method

1. Peel and chop the onion.
2. Slice the mushrooms.
3. Peel and crush or chop the garlic.
4. Heat the oil in a saucepan and fry the onion, garlic and mushrooms for 5 minutes.
5. Stir in the curry paste and tomato puree.
6. Add the chickpeas and coconut milk.
7. Simmer gently for 20 minutes.
8. Serve with pearl barley.

Other Options

- Use 400ml water and a Tbs of vegetable stock paste instead of coconut milk.
- Add other vegetables and pulses to the curry, e.g. courgettes, peas, red kidney beans.

MAHARAGWE
Serves 4

Ingredients

- 1 Tbs EVOO
- ½ onion, chopped
- ½ red pepper, chopped
- 2-3 cloves garlic, minced
- 2 tsp. ground turmeric
- 2 tsp. ground cumin
- 1 tsp. ground coriander
- ¼ tsp. ground cardamom
- Fat pinch crushed red pepper flakes
- 1 tsp. ginger paste
- 1 medium chilli, chopped
- Salt & pepper to taste
- 500g cooked beans or raw lentils (2 cans beans, drained)
- 1 can chopped tomatoes
- 1 can full-fat coconut milk

Notes

This traditional Kenyan dish can be made with any beans or lentils.

Method

1. Gently sauté onion, pepper, and garlic in EVOO in a big saucepan over medium heat until soft, 7-10 mins.
2. While the vegetables are cooking, measure out your spices into a small bowl and open your cans.
3. Add all spices, including the ginger paste and chopped chilli. Stir to create a paste-like consistency and cook about one minute, not allowing the mixture to get too dry (add a splash of water if needed).
4. Reduce heat to low and add salt and pepper, beans, tomatoes, and coconut milk. Add water to thin to desired consistency.
5. Simmer at least 20 mins, stirring occasionally. (If using raw lentils, cooking time will depend on the type.)

SEAFOOD 'RISOTTO'
Serves 4

Ingredients

- 2 Tbs EVOO
- 1 finely diced shallot or onion (100g)
- 2 cloves garlic – finely chopped
- 2 cups cooked **(or 1 cup raw)** pearl barley*
- 350g frozen mixed seafood
- 150g frozen peas
- 250ml **(or 400ml)** fish stock*
- Salt & Pepper to taste

Equipment

Large saucepan or pressure cooker

Notes

Make this on the hob with cooked barley or in a pressure cooker with raw.
The nutty barley makes a great replacement for rice.

Method

1. Put the oil into the pan and sauté the shallot for 2 minutes.
2. Add the garlic cook for half a minute.
3. Add all the other ingredients and bring to the boil.
4. Simmer for 5 minutes, to cook the seafood through.
5. Taste and adjust the seasoning.

Pressure cooker version: (quantities in brackets)*

1. Gently sauté the shallot in the oil for 5 minutes, add the garlic and cook for a further minute, then add a cup of **raw** barley and 400ml of fish stock & stir well.
2. Pressure cook for 24 minutes.
3. Release the pressure and stir in the mixed seafood and peas.
4. Pressure cook for 1 minute & quick realese the pressure.
5. Stir, season and serve.

LENTIL & MUSHROOM 'RISOTTO'
Serves 4

Ingredients

- 20 g dried porcini
- 2 Tbs Extra Virgin Olive Oil
- 1 finely diced shallot
- 200g raw pearl barley
- 4 cloves garlic
- 200g brown/green lentils
- 1L stock
- 200g mushrooms
- 100g frozen peas
- Salt & Pepper to taste
- a handful of chopped parsley & squeeze of lemon to finish.

Equipment

Large saucepan

Notes

You can cook this in a pressure cooker and it takes 15 minutes from step 6. (reduce the stock by 50ml)

Method

1. Soak the porcini in a cup of boiling water (250ml).
2. Put the oil into the pan and sauté the shallot for 1 minute.
3. Add finely chopped garlic and the raw barley and toast for 1 minute.
4. Add the stock, bring to the boil, cover and simmer for 15 minutes. (I use water and a Tbs of my homemade stock paste. See p54 for recipe).
5. Drain the porcini, keeping the soaking liquid. Roughly chop the porcini and add it to the pan. Add the soaking liquid, leaving any grit in the bottom of the cup.
6. Add the chopped mushrooms & lentils & season well.
7. Stir well and simmer for another 30 minutes.
8. 3 minutes before the end, add the peas and allow to heat through.
9. Add chopped parsley a squeeze of lemon, stir, taste & season before serving.

PRESSURE COOKER SEAFOOD 'PASTA'
Serves 4

Ingredients

- 1 Tbs Extra Virgin Olive Oil
- Half an onion, finely chopped
- 3 cloves garlic, chopped
- 2 cups yellow pea pasta (160g)
- 1/2 tsp chilli flakes or a chopped fresh chilli
- 300g frozen mixed seafood
- 1 tin chopped tomatoes
- 16 black olives (optional)
- 1 Tbs capers (optional)

Equipment

Pressure Cooker

Notes

Any pasta can be used, just cook for half the packet time.

Method

1. Heat the oil in the pressure cooker and add the chopped onion and sauté gently for 3 minutes.
2. Add the chopped garlic & sauté for a further minute.
3. Add the pasta and enough water to **almost** cover it.
4. Add the mixed seafood and seasoning.
5. Put the tinned tomatoes on top of everything and season well.
6. Pressure cook for 4 minutes. (or a minute under half the packet time)
7. Quick release, to stop the cooking.
8. If you like them, add halved olives and capers, stir through and serve.

*If you don't have a pressure cooker, follow the same method but cook the mixture for the time on the pasta packet. You will need to add an extra 100ml of liquid, too.

STIR FRY

This meal can be made large or small
and as varied as you like.
All the preparation is done first
and then it's all cooked together.
You can be as creative as you like!

You could include:
- Thinly sliced onion
- Finely chopped garlic (or garlic paste)
- Finely chopped ginger (or ginger paste)
- Finely chopped lemon grass
- Thinly sliced bell peppers – all colours
- Finely diced chilli
- Courgette ribbons – made with a potato peeler
- Carrot ribbons – made with a potato peeler
- Sliced mushrooms of all types
- Finely shredded cabbage or Brussel sprouts
- Sprouts – home-grown or shop bought bean sprouts
- Water chestnuts – available in tins
- Bamboo shoots – available in tins
- Green beans or mange tout – halved lengthways
- Baby sweetcorn
- Broccoli or cauliflower in small florets

Traditional Method

1. In a wok or large frying pan, heat 2 tablespoons of oil: Extra Virgin Olive Oil, rapeseed or avocado oil are good.
2. Add the ginger, garlic & lemon grass if using & stir briskly for one minute.
3. Add the more dense vegetables first and move them around the hot pan briskly for 3 or 4 minutes, now add the smaller or more delicate vegetables, such as the bean sprouts or courgette ribbons.
4. Stir these some more for a few minutes, then add the soy sauce or coconut aminos – around 1 Tbs per serving.
5. Sprinkle liberally with around a level teaspoon per serving of Chinese 5 spice powder & continue to stir everything for another 3 or 4 minutes.
6. If it's getting too hot, add a couple of tablespoons of water or Chinese Rice Wine (Shaoxing)
7. If using precooked protein, add it now, stir everything through & allow to heat through for 2 or 3 minutes.
8. Serve, topped with a drizzle of sesame oil & a sprinkle of sesame seeds, chopped peanuts or cashews.

* If adding meat or raw seafood, cut into small strips & cook it before hand in some hot oil. Make sure it's cooked all the way through. Take it out & keep it warm to one side, while you cook everything else.

Air Fryer Method

You can really easily cook a version of a stir fry in an air fryer that has a big drawer.

1. Simply prepare all your ingredients by pre cooking your meat or seafood & chopping all your vegetables, then toss the vegetables in 2 Tablespoons of oil per serving.
2. Pre-heat the air fryer to 180°C
3. Then put the vegetables in the drawer & cook for 10 minutes.
4. After 10 minutes, give everything a really good stir and shake. Make sure you turn everything over.
5. Turn the temperature up to 200°C & cook for a further 10 minutes.
6. If adding meat or seafood, add it now and heat through for a further 3-5 minutes.
7. Add the soy sauce & Chinese 5 Spice and stir it through really well.
8. Serve, topped with a drizzle of sesame oil & a sprinkle of sesame seeds, chopped peanuts or cashews.

BAKED FISH

Ingredients

Per portion:
- A fish fillet: cod, salmon, haddock, coley.
- A sprig of rosemary or thyme.
- A slice of lemon
- A glug of good olive oil Salt & Pepper
- A glug of white wine (optional)

Equipment

Tin foil
Oven-proof container

Notes

You can bake this fish in the oven or in an air fryer. You can also mix up the herbs however you like

Method

1. Preheat your oven to 180° C
2. Tear off a large sheet of foil, more than three times the size of your fish.
3. Place it on a plate and put your fish fillet on top.
4. Place the lemon, rosemary, oil, salt & pepper on top.
5. Bring the sides of the foil up to make a parcel, sealed on three sides, by turning the edges over onto each other at least twice.
6. If using wine, turn up the open end of your parcel, add the wine, then seal the last edge.
7. Pop in your hot oven or air fryer for 20 minutes.
8. Open very carefully as the parcel will be full of delicious sauce to go on your fish portion.
    *You can wrap 2 portions in one parcel.

CHACHOUKA WITH EGGS
Serves 2

Ingredients

- 3 Tbs Extra Virgin Olive Oil
- 1 tsp cumin seeds
- 1 large onion, halved and thinly sliced
- 2 bell peppers finely sliced
- 1/2 tsp hot smoked paprika
- A pinch of saffron
- a tin of chopped tomatoes
- 4 eggs

Equipment

Large saucepan or pressure cooker

Notes

Duck eggs are really good in this recipe. Add a couple of minutes to be sure that they're cooked.

Method

1. Heat the olive oil, add the cumin seeds and gently fry them for a couple of minutes.
2. Add the onion and cook slowly for 8-10 minutes, until soft and golden.
3. Add the garlic and peppers and cook over a low heat for 20 minutes, until the peppers are soft.
4. Add the paprika, saffron, tomatoes, salt and pepper.
5. Cook for a further 15 minutes, taste and adjust seasoning.
6. Now make 4 wells in the mixture and crack an egg into each hole, cover the pan and leave on low for 5-6 minutes to cook the eggs through.
Pressure Cooker Method: After softening the onions, add all the other ingredients (apart from the eggs) & pressure cook for 7 minutes. Add the eggs & cover for 5 - 6 minutes until eggs are cooked

CHICKEN TIKKA MARINADE

Ingredients

- 1 Tbsp of lemon juice
- 2 tsp of ginger paste (or fresh minced)
- 2 tsp of garlic paste (or fresh minced)
- 1 pinch of salt
- 1 tsp red chilli powder
- 100g of natural yoghurt
- 1/2 tsp turmeric powder
- 1/2 tsp garam masala
- 20ml of oil

Equipment

baking tray,
oven,
air fryer
or frying pan

Notes

You can marinade any meat, seafood or vegetable in this delicious paste.

Method

1. Mix the marinade ingredients together in a large jug or bowl.
2. Add chicken pieces and stir to coat well. (4 chicken thighs or 2 breasts, cut into strips).
4. Cover and refrigerate over night, or at least a few hours.
5. Place on the tray or in the airfryer basket.
6. Bake at 180°C for 18-20 minutes.
7. Check the internal temperature is over 75°C or test that a thicker piece of meat is cooked all the way through.

* For a more authentic recipe, marinade the chicken first in lemon juice, garlic & ginger for 20 minutes, then add the other ingredients and marinade overnight.

SALADE NIÇOISE
2 SERVINGS

Ingredients

- A handful of lettuce leaves
- 200g cooked green beans, halved
- 6 boiled new potatoes, halved or quartered
- 4 cherry tomatoes, halved
- 2 Boiled eggs, quartered
- 8 black olives, halved
- 10 capers
- 2 artichoke hearts, quartered
- 1 tin of tuna in spring water
- vinaigrette (see p56)

Equipment

A large salad bowl

Notes

This is my simplified version of a delicious traditional French salad

Method

1. Rinse and dry the lettuce leaves & line the salad bowl with them.
2. Add the new potatoes, green beans, black olives, artichoke pieces and any spare lettuce leaves, roughly chopped. Mix together, without disturbing the outer leaves too much.
3. Drain the tuna and flake it on top of the salad.
4. Decorate the bowl with the quartered eggs and season with salt and pepper.
5. Drizzle with vinaigrette dressing.
6. To serve, toss everything together and put half on each plate, ensuring both servings have plenty of everything.

*You can also add some chopped anchovies, if you like them.

CAULIFLOWER CHEESE/ MACARONI CHEESE
Serves 2

Ingredients

- Cauliflower OR 100g yellow bean pasta
- 300g silken tofu
- 125g grated Cheddar cheese
- 1 heaped Tbs chick-pea flour
- 1 tsp Mustard
- salt and pepper

Equipment

whisk
2 saucepans

Notes

You can use any type of pasta for this recipe or any vegetable!

Method

1. Cook the pasta in plenty of boiling water according to the packet instructions. (Set a timer)
2. OR steam, pressure cook or microwave the cauliflower.
3. Heat 100g of the cheese & all the other ingredients **gently** in a saucepan and whisk to make a smooth sauce. Do not boil as it may split. (For pasta, I like to add a handful of frozen mixed vegetables at this point).
4. Strain the pasta or cauliflower & place in an oven proof dish.
5. Pour the sauce over liberally and top with the reserved 25g of cheese and another grind of pepper.
6. Grill or air fry to brown the top.
   *For a simple pouring sauce, omit the chick-pea flour but do not bake as the sauce will split.

EASY RATATOUILLE
Serves 2

Ingredients

- 1 Tbs Extra Virgin Olive Oil
- 2 cloves garlic
- 1 large courgette
- 1 red pepper
- 1 red onion
- 1 aubergine
- 100g tomatoes
- 100g mushrooms
- 1/2 tsp Herbes de Provence or oregano
- Salt & Pepper
- 16 black olives (optional)
- 1 Tbs capers (optional)

Equipment

Pressure cooker or large saucepan

Notes

This is an easy version of a French classic dish. Add eggs or a handful of red lentils to make it a full meal.

Method

1. Cut everything into roughly the same size pieces: Halve and slice the courgettes, cut the pepper into bite-sized chunks, roughly chop the onion, slice and cube the aubergine, quarter or halve the mushrooms and tomatoes.
2. Heat the oil and add the chopped onion and the crushed or chopped garlic and cook gently for 4 or 5 minutes until the onion pieces are soft.
3. Add all the other ingredients and give them a good stir.
4. If **pressure cooking**, close the lid and pressure cook for 2 minutes, quick release.
5. In a **saucepan**, cover and simmer for 10 -15 minutes until everything is soft.
6. Season to taste.

EASY PARMIGIANA MELANZANE
Serves 1

Ingredients

- 2 slices aubergine
- 2 Tbs Extra Virgin Olive Oil
- 2 Tbs tomato purée
- 2 tomatoes
- 2 mushrooms
- 150g mozzarella (or other cheese)
- 1 tsp oregano
- salt & pepper

Equipment

Grill, oven or air fryer
Baking tray
Pastry brush

Notes

This is a totally inauthentic, quick version of an Italian classic.

Method

1. Preheat your oven, grill or air fryer to 200°C
2. Brush one side of each slice of aubergine with olive oil. (If you don't have a brush, use a spoon, your fingers or a folded piece of kitchen roll.)
3. Cook the oiled side for 5 minutes.
4. Meanwhile slice all the vegetables quite thinly, so that they will sit comfortably on the aubergine slices.
5. Turn each slice over and oil the other side. Cook for another 5 minutes.
6. Remove from the oven/grill/air fryer and spread each slice with the tomato purée.
7. Layer the vegetables on each slice and cover with the cheese and seasoning.
8. Squash down to hold everything in place.
9. Cook for a further 5 minutes until the cheese has melted.

COURGETTI FASTONARA
Serves 2

Ingredients

- 2 courgettes
- 100g mushrooms
- 60g cream cheese
- 2 tsp olive oil
- 20g grated parmesan
- Black pepper
- *10g finely chopped herbs, such as chives, coriander or parsley (optional)

Equipment

spiraliser
large frying pan

Notes

This was originally a 5:2 fasting meal, but is really delicious as a meal or a side dish.

Method

1. Cut the mushrooms into quarters and cook them in the pan with the olive oil. Don't move them around to much, so that they get nicely caramelised.
2. Meanwhile, spiralise the courgettes or use a potato peeler to make them into ribbons.
3. Tip the mushrooms out of the pan and add the courgettes to it. Cook them for a couple of minutes.
4. Return the cooked mushrooms to the pan and add the cream cheese, parmesan and black pepper to taste.
5. Give it all a good stir and gently warm through.
6. Serve with an extra twist of black pepper and finely chopped herbs if using.

COURGETTE AND STILTON SOUP
(makes 1.4L)

Ingredients

- 2 Tbs EVOO
- 500g courgettes
- 2 medium onions
- 750ml stock (or 500ml water & a Tbs of veg stock paste from p54)
- 150g Stilton
- 1 tsp oregano
- salt and pepper

Equipment

Pressure cooker
or large saucepan
blender or hand blender

Notes

This is a really easy
soup to batch cook and
freeze in portions.

Method

1. Roughly dice the onion and gently fry it in the olive oil.
2. Meanwhile halve and slice the courgettes into chunks.
3. When the onion is soft, add the courgettes and oregano and stir well for 3-5 minutes to brown a little.
4. Add the stock, and seasoning. Either pressure cook for 2 minutes or simmer for 10, until the courgettes are cooked through.
5. Chop the Stilton into small cubes or crumble, and add it to the hot soup.
6. Leave to melt for 3-5 minutes then blend to your preferred consistency.

ROASTED RED PEPPER & TOMATO SOUP
(makes 1.6L)

Ingredients

- 2 red peppers
- 8 medium sized tomatoes
- 1 red chilli or a big pinch of chilli powder
- 1 Tbs Extra Virgin Olive Oil
- Pinch of ground black pepper
- 750ml stock (or water & 1 dessert-spoon veg stock paste from p54).

Equipment

baking tray, large saucepan with lid, measuring jug measuring spoons, hand blender/blender

Notes

This is a tasty soup to batch cook and freeze in portions.

Method

1. Put the oven on at 190°C or preheat your air fryer.
2. Chop the peppers into bite size pieces.
3. Place them onto a baking tray, season & sprinkle with the olive oil.
4. Put them into the oven or aor fryer for 15 minutes, until lightly roasted.
5. Chop the tomatoes into quarters.
5. Put the water, tomatoes, chilli, and stock into a saucepan.
6. Bring to boiling point, and then simmer with a lid on for 10 minutes. (Or pressure cook for 2 minutes).
7. Add the roasted peppers to the mixture and simmer for a further 2 minutes.
7. Briefly purée the soup with a hand blender.
8. Serve & enjoy!

PEA & MINT SOUP
(makes 1.4L)

Ingredients

- 1 stalk celery chopped
- 1 medium onion chopped
- 1/2 clove garlic chopped or crushed
- 750 ml stock (or water & 1 Tbs of vegetable stock paste p54)
- 400g fresh or frozen peas
- a sprig of fresh mint
- black pepper to taste

Equipment

Saucepan, measuring jug, weighing scales

Notes

A super convenient soup that can be made with frozen peas

Method

1. Add the chopped celery, onion, garlic and peas to the pan. (If you are using frozen peas there is no need to defrost them).
2. Add the stock (or water & stock paste) and bring to the boil.
3. Reduce the heat, put the lid on and simmer for about 15 minutes. (Or pressure cook for 2 minutes).
4. Meanwhile pick the leaves from the bunch of mint, discard the stalks and chop the leaves finely.
5. When the peas have softened, remove the pan from heat, season with salt and pepper and add the chopped mint.
6. Using a blender (or hand blender) blend until smooth.
7. Garnish with a sprig of fresh mint and enjoy!

ROAST MEDITERRANEAN VEGETABLES

Ingredients

For 2 large portions:
- 1 red pepper
- 1 red onion
- 6 mushrooms
- 3 cloves of garlic
- 1 courgette
- 6 cherry tomatoes
- 1 Tbs olive oil
- Salt, pepper & oregano

Equipment

Large baking tray
Oven or air fryer

Notes

This mixture freezes well and is great as a side dish, with eggs or omelette

Method

1. Cut all the vegetables into roughly equal sized chunks: quarter the mushrooms, slice the courgette into thick rings, peel the onion and cut into 6 or 8 chunks or wedges, leave the tomatoes whole & the garlic cloves whole and in their skins.
2. Put all the vegetables, olive oil and seasoning in a large bowl and stir well to coat everything.
3. Spread the oiled vegetables out on a baking tray or in your air fryer basket.
4. Cook for 20-30 minutes, stirring, turning or shaking half way.

* Squeeze the garlic out of its skins for a tasty treat!
* If you like it spicy, you can add a whole hot chilli or two to the mixture.

VEGETABLE STOCK PASTE

Ingredients

- 700g vegetables/trimmings
- 2 garlic cloves
- a handful of fresh herbs
- 100g rock salt
- 1 Tbs olive oil
- 1 Tbs apple cider vinegar
- 1 tsp turmeric
* Parmesan rind (optional)

Equipment

Pressure cooker or large pan, blender

Notes

I freeze vegetable scraps until I have enough to make a batch of paste. It freezes well & can be used straight from the freezer.

Method

1. Cut the vegetables into rough chunks, peel the garlic cloves and add all ingredients, apart from the parmesan rinds, to your pressure cooker or large pan.
2. Pressure cook for 10 minutes or simmer in the pan for 30 minutes, until everything is soft.
3. If using parmesan rinds, blend them to a powder and add to the cooked mixture.
4. Blend the mixture to a smooth paste.
5. Place into small containers and allow to cool before freezing.
6. Be sure to label the containers and use the paste from frozen whenever a recipe calls for stock. *Remember that it contains a lot of salt (which acts as a preservative) so you may not need to add extra salt when cooking with it.

GUACAMOLE

Ingredients

- ¼ small red onion, peeled
- a small handful of fresh coriander (about 10g)
- 1 tomato, cut into quarters or smaller if mashing,
- 2 large ripe avocados, peeled
- 1 tablespoon of lime juice + more to taste
- 1 Jalapeño, sliced (optional)
- salt to taste

Equipment

Food processor
Blender or masher

Method

Simply blend everything together in a food processor or mash with a fork to your preferred consistency.

Serve with seedy crackers (p63) or raw vegetables to dip Also great on top of any salad.

Optional extras;

- Garlic
- Cumin
- Tabasco sauce
- Basil

VINAIGRETTE

Ingredients

- 6 Tbs Extra Virgin Olive Oil
- 2 Tbs Apple Cider Vinegar
- 2 tsp mustard
- salt & pepper to taste

Equipment

Jam jar with lid

Notes

This simple vinaigrette can be made in the jar and stored in the fridge. You can change up the oil, use lemon juice, pomegranate syrup, add garlic, miso or your choice of herbs.

Method

Jar Method

Place all the ingredients in the jar, shake, taste and season.

Fork Method

This makes a thicker, emulsified sauce.

1. Put the olive oil and mustard into a bowl.
2. Whisk together with a fork until emulsified – this can take 2 or 3 minutes.
3. Add the other ingredients, mix well and season to taste.

BLENDER MAYONNAISE

Ingredients
- 1 egg
- 2 tsp Dijon mustard
- juice of half a lemon
- 350ml oil
  (I use avocado oil)
- salt and pepper

Equipment
Hand Blender
Tall jar

Notes
You can add all sorts of flavourings to this mayonnaise afterwards, like garlic or chopped herbs.
Store it in a sealed container in the fridge for up to a week.

Method

1. Carefully place the egg into a tall container taking care not to crack the yolk.
2. Add the mustard, lemon juice and seasoning
3. Gently pour the oil on top.
4. Now put your stick blender into the container to cover the egg yolk and turn it on.
5. You'll see the mixture emulsify and go cloudy.
6. Now gently raise the blender through the mixture and back down again a couple of times to incorporate all the oil. This only takes a few seconds.
7. Taste and adjust the seasoning and add lemon juice if necessary.

CASHEW MAYONNAISE

Ingredients

- 60g Cashew nuts
- 60 ml water
- 2 Tbs lemon juice
- 1/2 tsp Dijon mustard
- a good pinch of salt

Equipment

Blender

Notes

Simple, vegan, high protein & delicious!

Method

1. Place all the ingredients into a blender and blend until smooth and creamy.
2. You may need to scrape down and blend a few times to get the texture really smooth.
3. Taste and adjust seasoning.

   Keeps in the fridge for up to 3 days.

PESTO

Ingredients

- 80g fresh basil
- 50g toasted pine nuts
- 50g Parmesan (roughly chopped)
- 150ml Extra Virgin Olive Oil
- 2 cloves garlic – peeled

Equipment

Blender

Notes

See p13 for lots of pesto variety ideas.

Method

1. Add all the ingredients to a blender:
2. Whizz until smooth
3. Season to taste.
4. Store in the fridge or freezer.

GREMOLATA

Ingredients

- 30g flat-leaf parsley, leaves and stalks
- 2 garlic cloves, peeled
- 2 unwaxed lemons, zested and ½ lemon, juiced
- 1 Tbsp extra virgin olive oil

Equipment

Zester, fine grater, juicer

Notes

This zingy 'dressing' is delicious on top of fish or salad, cooked vegetables, hummus or anything that needs a boost.

Method

1. Finely chop the parsley.
2. Finely grate the garlic.
3. Mix together with the lemon zest and juice in a bowl.
4. Stir in the oil.
5. More oil can be added if you prefer a looser consistency.

ROMESCO SAUCE

Ingredients
- 1 red pepper
- 1 Tbs lemon juice
- 1 Tbs sherry vinegar
- 130g EVOO
- 1/4 clove garlic
- 2 long chillis
- 100g toasted pine nuts or almonds
- 2 tsp paprika
- 2 tsp ground cumin
- 2 pinches black pepper
- 2 pinches salt

Equipment
Grill
Bowl
Blender

Notes
This is particularly good with fish, but is a tasty addition to anything grilled.

Method

1. Char the pepper under grill or over a gas hob, until the skin blisters.(10-15 minutes) (You could also use a jar of roasted red peppers).
2. Place it into a bowl and cover with cling film. After 10 minutes the skin will be loose and easy to peel off with your hands.
3. Place the flesh of the pepper and all the other ingredients in a blender and blend to a paste.

* I like mine with a bit of texture, so I pulse it to a coarser blend.

SPICY CHICK PEAS

Ingredients

- 250g cooked chick peas (tinned are fine)
- 1 Tbs olive or avocado oil
- 1 tsp paprika
- 1 tsp salt
- 1/2 tsp cumin
- 1/2 tsp coriander

Equipment

Oven or air fryer

Notes

These make a great snack with a glass of wine or a topping for other dishes. You can change the spices to suit your taste.

Method

1. Dry the chick peas over night on some kitchen paper. (This is optional but will make them more crunchy and quicker to crisp up).
2. Place in a jug or bowl with the oil, salt and spices.
3. Stir to coat well
4. Place well spread out in an oven tray, on an air fryer shelf or basket.
5. Cook at 200°C for 20 – 30 minutes.

* You can use tinned chickpeas or dried ones that you have cooked yourself (much cheaper).
* You cn also use cooked lentils & roast for 30 minutes.

61

SEEDY BESAN CRACKERS

Ingredients

- 1 cup of mixed seeds. I use sunflower, pumpkin, sesame, flax & chopped pine nuts.
- 3 Tbs Chick pea flour
- 2 Tbs Nutritional Yeast
- 1 tsp dried herbs
- 1/2 tsp chilli flakes
- 1/2 tsp salt
- 2 Tbs Extra Virgin Olive Oil
- 4 Tbs hot tap water

Equipment
Large bowl
Large tray
Parchment paper

Notes
You can use any blend of seeds and add any herbs and spices that you like.

Method

1. Preheat your oven to 160°C
2. In a bowl mix all the ingredients together to a firm dough.
3. Roll the mixture out between 2 sheets or parchment paper. (it will be sticky)
4. Peel off the top sheet and bake in your hot oven for 30 minutes or until dry & slightly golden.
5. Break into cracker sized shards & store in an airtight tin.
6. Enjoy dipped in guacamole (p55), Hummus (p31) or serve with cheese.

CHAFFLES

Ingredients

- 2 Tbsp ground almonds
- ½ tsp baking powder
- 60g mozzarella/cheddar grated
- 1 large egg
- oil for greasing

Equipment

Waffle maker
Mixing bowl

Notes

There are many variations of chaffles on the internet. Have fun experimenting.

Method

1. Put the waffle maker on to heat up.
2. Break the egg into the bowl and lightly whisk it.
3. Add the other ingredients and stir to combine.
4. Lightly oil the waffle maker.
5. When it's hot enough add enough mixture to almost fill half of the 'chamber'
6. Close the waffle maker and wait for the 'ready' light to come back on.
7. The time each chaffle takes will depend on the size and power of your waffle maker. Make sure it's fully cooked before you try to remove it.
8. Enjoy with toppings or as a side to any meal.

SWEETCORN PAKORA
Makes 16 - 20 Balls

Ingredients

- 200g Sweetcorn
- 2 spring onions, sliced
- 1 tsp chilli paste
- 1 tsp garlic paste
- 1 tsp ginger paste
- 50g roughly chopped mint or coriander
- 1 tsp ground cumin
- 1/2 tsp turmeric
- 2 Tbs (60g) of chick-pea flour,
- EVOO for frying

Equipment

Sharp knife,
Food processor or blender
Large bowl.
Frying pan

Notes

To make these extra spicy add extra fresh chilli.

Method

1. If using fresh garlic, ginger or chilli chop, crush or grate them to a smooth paste.
2. Add all the ingredients apart from the flour & oil in to a blender and pulse to make a coarse paste. You want to still see the sweetcorn kernels.
3. Add the chick pea flour and pulse again to make a sticky paste.
4. Make small balls or patties of the mixture, using about 2-3 tsp of mixture for each.
5. Cook them slowly, turning often, until they are golden.
6. Serve with a yoghurt mint & cucumber raita or a coriander, chilli and coconut dip.

*You can also add some chopped spinach to this mixture, just make sure that you squeeze it dry first.

TAHINI COOKIES
Makes 16 cookies

Ingredients
- 200g maple syrup
- 200g tahini
- 1 Tbs nut butter
- pinch of salt
- 2 tsp vanilla extract
- 220g ground almonds
- 2 Tbs pumpkin seeds
- 2 Tbs dark choc chips/ chopped dark chocolate
- Salt flakes for topping

Equipment

mixing bowl
baking tray
oven or air fryer

Notes

This indulgent recipe is from The Health Boost website.

Method

1. Preheat your oven to 170°
2. Add maple syrup, tahini, vanilla and nut butter to the bowl and mix thoroughly.
3. Fold in the ground almonds and salt and mix to a smooth paste..
4. Add the chocolate pieces and pumpkin seeds and mix well to make a sticky dough.
5. Make the dough into 16 small balls. (I use a small ice cream scoop, then roll with wet hands).
6. Place on a baking sheet and gently press down.
7. Sprinkle with any extra pumpkin seeds and sea salt.
8. Bake for 15-20 minutes, until golden.
9. Allow to fully cool before eating.

FLAX SEED CHOCOLATE COOKIES

Ingredients

- 2 Tbs milled flaxseed
- 3 Tbs brown sugar
- 3 Tbs EVOO
- 200g ground almonds
- 50g chopped pecans, walnuts or other nuts
- 60g dark chocolate, drops or chopped into chunks.
- pinch of salt

Equipment

small bowl
large bowl
brownie tray
greaseproof paper
oven or air fryer

Notes

This is based on the ZOE Instagram post recipe for individual cookies

Method

1. Put your oven on at 180°C
2. In a small bowl, mix the ground flaxseed with 4Tbs water and set aside.
3. In a large bowl, mix together the oil & sugar.
4. Once the flaxseed has absorbed all the water, add it to the oil and sugar and mix well.
5. Add all the other ingredients and combine well. (you can do this gently, in a blender).
6. Line the tray with greaseproof paper and press the mixture firmly into the tray, spreading it evenly.
7. Bake for 15-20 minutes, until the top looks crisp.
8. Remove from the oven, and while warm, score into small squares.
9. Remove from the pan and allow to cool on a cooling rack.

ALMOND FLOUR PANCAKES

Ingredients

- 125g ground almonds
- 75g chick-pea flour
- 1 teaspoon baking powder
- big pinch of sea salt
- 120g milk, kefir or yoghurt
- 1 tablespoon honey
- 1 teaspoon vanilla
- 2 large eggs
- Flavourless oil, for frying (I use avocado)

Equipment

Blender
Mixing bowl
Whisk
Frying pan

Notes

This batter makes thick pancakes that are perfect served with yoghurt and fruit. Microwave for 20 seconds to reheat.

Method

1. Separate the eggs & blend the yolks and all the other batter ingredients together.
2. Your batter needs to be slightly thicker than double cream so add more liquid or flour if necessary.
3. In a clean mixing bowl, whisk the egg whites to stiff peaks.
4. Mix 2 Tbs of whipped egg whites into the batter to loosen the mixture, then carefully fold in the remaining egg whites to make a light, fluffy batter.
5. Heat a pan over medium-low heat. Brush the pan with a little flavourelss oil and when it is hot, add a tablespoon of batter for each pancake.
6. Cook the pancakes slowly for 1 to 2 minutes per side, turning the heat to low as needed so that the middles cook without burning the outsides.
7. Serve warm with yoghurt and fresh or frozen fruit.

Appendix 1 - Links & Resources

Delicious condiments without additives
www. Condimaniac.com

Everything Sour dough
www.foodbodsourdough.com

Crowd Farming - Great ingredients direct from producers
www.CrowdFarming.com

Getting People Growing - Seed growing kits
www.gettingpeoplegrowing.co.uk

Glucose Goddess - great advice on eating for better health
www.glucosegoddess.com

Appendix 2 - Useful Facebook Groups

Fresher Bites

UK Fermenting Friends

Sourdough with foodbod

Love Food, Eat Healthy

UK Companies I love:

Honestly Tasty - Amazing nut based 'cheeses'

Wild & Game - frozen game meat delivered

Appendix 3 - Podcasts

Zoe - Science & Nutrition

The Doctor's Kitchen Podcast

Intermittent Fasting Stories - Gin Stephens

Intermittent Fasting For L*IF*E with Gin & Sheri

Appendix 4 – Pressure cooking times for pulses.

- Dried beans double in weight & volume when cooked, so be sure to less than half fill your pressure cooker.

- Use enough liquid to cover the beans well.

- Soaking is not necessary, but as you can see from the chart, it can save a lot of time and fuel. Ideally soak them overnight, but 6-8 hours may be sufficient.

Dried Beans & Legumes	Dry Cooking Time (minutes)	Soaked Cooking Time (minutes)
Black Beans	20–25	4–6
Black Eyed Peas	6–7	4–5
Chickpeas (Garbanzo)	35–40	10–15
Cannelini	25–30	6–9
Pigeon Peas	20–25	6–9
Lentils – Puy	4–6	N/A
Lentils – Green, Brown, Mini, Beluga	4–6	N/A
Lentils – Red Split	1–2	N/A
Lentils – Yellow split (moong dal)	1–2	N/A
Butter Beans (Lima)	12–14	3–6
Kidney Beans– red	15–20	7–8
Haricot Beans (Navy)	20–25	7–8
Pinto Beans	23–25	6–9
Peas	16–20	10–12
Soy Beans	35–40	18–20

HELLO ZOE!

I took part in some research by ZOE Science & Nutrition, and discovered that my super healthy diet, was actually lacking in quite a few areas.

My body personally copes badly with both glucose and fats and ZOE's guidelines gave me information about which foods would be better for my body in both the short and long term, I have used their guidance to make some changes, both large and small, which I hope you can benefit from, regardless of how well your own body processes different foods.

I have added a vast array of plants to my diet, in the form of vegetables, seeds, nuts, herbs and spices. Not only are these delicious, but modern research shows that eating at least 30 types of plant a week is really good for our gut microbiome, and consequently for our overall health. Some of my ideas are specifically aimed at adding variety to your diet and I propose that you just pick one idea a week and try it out.

One of the biggest changes is that I have reduced my intake of wheat, rice and potatoes. I know that sounds extreme, but I have found a great number of tasty replacements, that add flavour, fibre and protein whilst reducing my carbohydrate intake.

All these things not only add to my pleasure in eating but also reduce my risk of type 2 diabetes, heart disease and even many cancers. I've lost some menopause weight and find that I can eat a lot without gaining it back.

I hope you experience some of these benefits, too.

Printed in Great Britain
by Amazon